AXOLOTL

AN EASY AND UNDERSTANDABLE GUIDE TO KEEPING AND CARING FOR AXOLOTL(HOUSING, FEEDING, TREATING, AND BREEDING)

Table of Contents

Introduction

Thank you for choosing this book. This easy and understandable guide will explain everything you need to know anout the axolotl pet. The axolotl is strictly aquatic. It never leaves the water. It generally evolves by walking or crawling on the ground. Sometimes it rests by floating on the surface or by resting on an element of the scenery or on a plant. It hardly swims, except when, disturbed, a reflex of escape propels it quickly forward by powerful movements of the tail and undulations of the body, the legs tightened along the body. When it uses its air breathing, for example when the water becomes more or too hot, less rich in oxygen, it gains the surface to take a gulp of air. To activate the use of its external gills, it moves them by jerks.

Its sight seems rather reduced, it seeks its food on the ground, with the touch, the smell or the taste thanks to receptors located on the tongue, and in the mouth. Detection is based on the movement of the food or on the smell of the food after the animals have been accustomed to inert food. It occurs only at short distance, a few centimeters. The capture of the food is a reflex movement of aspiration, violent and not very precise. The animal does not chew, it sucks the whole prey, the teeth are just used to retain the piece of food. Animals that are looking for food typically stand with their heads slightly tilted downwards or obliquely to the ground. Apart from reproduction, and as long as they are too large to be considered as prey, the axolotl shows no interest in its fellow animals, no social activity, no territorial behavior. However, as the taking of food is a blind reflex, it can happen that it seizes by accident a piece of leg, gill or another part of another axolotl and sometimes tears it off. The damaged part can be reconstituted.

Axolotls have their home in stagnant waters and lakes near Mexico City, so they do not like water flows. They usually stay close to the bottom or directly on the bottom. In a home tank, too, it can usually be observed that axolotls feel most comfortable at the bottom.

As axolotls are nocturnal, many of the animals like to stay somewhat hidden during the day and only come out in the evening.

It is therefore good for the plants if a suitable lamp is also purchased for the tank. The lamp promotes good growth of the aquatic plants and prevents too many algae from settling in the tank. The light of the lamp should be white, not blue. Happy Reading.

Chapter 1: All about axolotls

Axolotls (***Ambystoma mexicanum***) are caudata amphibians but are often mistakenly thought to be reptiles. They are classified in the family of the mole salamanders (***genus Ambystoma***). Both size and expected lifespan can vary greatly in some cases. As a rule, axolotls grow to between 15 and 30 centimetres (***between 6 and 12 inches***) and weigh between 50 and 300 grams (***between 2 and 10 ounces***). However, there are also specimens that grow up to 40 centimetres (***16 inches***).

Most axolotls live between ten and twenty years. Occasionally, however, some axolotls have been known to live up to 25 years.

Axolotls need cool and oxygen-rich water. They are not solitary animals and should therefore be kept at least in pairs. Many owners decide to keep three animals. These should be about the same size!

Axolotls have external gills, and their lungs are not fully developed. Although they can switch between land and water for short periods, they should spend their lives in water as they are not adult moles but remain in the larval stage. The colder it is, the more often axolotls voluntarily go ashore.

Atl means **water** and *Xolotl* stands for **monster** but is also the name of an Aztec god. Axolotls probably got the name **water monster** because of their appearance, although nowadays many people find the little amphibians very cute and not monster-like.

Axolotls have their home in Mexico and are not too common in the wild. They lived in Lake Chalco, Lake Xochimilco and a few other bodies of water in Mexico. These are mainly stagnant waters and lakes.

The lakes mentioned are located in a volcanic basin near Mexico City. Today, they are largely dry, and the water bodies are only sparsely developed.

In 1805, Alexander von Humboldt, a German explorer, returned from an expedition in Mexico and brought back two axolotls. He wanted to study them more closely. Many years later, in 1863, a French research team brought a somewhat larger group of axolotls from Mexico to France. Over the years, the little animals were studied more and more intensively before they established themselves much later as popular pets.

The heads of axolotls are rounded and large, their limbs are relatively short. The eyes are wide apart. Behind the eyes they each have three gill branches that can be actively moved. Their tail is flat, has fin seams and is very long. Axolotls use their tail to control their swimming direction. Usually, the males have a slightly longer tail than the females.

What is special about axolotls is that although they grow steadily and also become reproductively mature, they always remain larvae. This peculiarity of axolotls is due to their limited thyroid function - hormones are produced in the thyroid gland of a living creature that are responsible, among other things, for the development of a larvae into an adult. Axolotls, however, have a malfunctioning thyroid gland, which is why they never become a 'proper' adult amphibian. Metamorphosis is therefore not possible for them. Through the external addition of artificial hormones, an axolotl can indeed develop into an adult caudate and then have a similar appearance to a tiger salamander, but this should be avoided. While an axolotl can live for ten to twenty years as a larva, it can only live for about five years if artificial hormones are administered. Life expectancy is therefore drastically shortened.

The permanent state in the larval stage is called neoteny. Although axolotls always remain larvae, they can of course reproduce.

Axolotls can regenerate their bodies very well and usually completely, as they are able to regrow their limbs, organs and even brain parts. How this is possible is still not fully understood. Research into the regenerative properties of axolotls is still ongoing. It is hoped that the research results and findings can also be applied in human medicine. However, some things have already been discovered. Axolotls have connective tissue cells that virtually reverse their development. The special body cells **fibroblasts** develop again into precursor cells that can form bones as well as skin and tendons. Thus, the regeneration of different types of connective tissue is possible. However, the adaptation to humans is proving difficult in research - humans also have fibroblasts. In the case of an injury, however, the human fibroblasts do not develop back into precursor cells, but they continue to develop into myofibroblasts - and these form the scar tissue in humans.

The genome of an axolotl is extremely complex. It is ten times as large as the genome of a human, as it has over thirty billion base pairs. Therefore, decoding this genome is not easy. However, it has already been researched that axolotls have some genes that are only found in them and other amphibian species. These genes are active in regenerating tissue.

The axolotl breathes in addition to atmospheric air thanks to a pair of rudimentary lungs, and, like all amphibians, it also breathes through the skin, which is devoid of scales and covered with a protective film, the mucus. It is a vital necessity, we will take care to always maintain an access to the air, notably in the bags of transport. Therefore, the skin is a particularly sensitive organ, exposed to diseases, to the effects of the degradation of the quality of the water etc... and its aspect is a good indicator of health.

The axolotl has four legs each carrying 4 (in front) or 5 clawed fingers (in the back). The sexual and excretory organs, not differentiated externally (the cloaca) are located between the back legs and the birth of the crest. The natural form is pigmented, grey speckled or mottled with black or more rarely brown-beige speckled with dark brown, with a lighter belly.

An adult Axolotl can measure anywhere from six to 18 inches. However, the usual size for this species is only nine inches. As for its weight, the males can weigh about 125 to 135 grams while the females can weigh about 170 to 180 grams – the females are usually bigger than the males.

The head of an Axolotl is wide – much like typical salamanders. Their eyes are lidless (unlike human eyes), so they can't blink their eyes (this is common in different types of fish as well).

As for their limbs, they have four short legs with long, thin digits. Their digits are what you would call fingers and toes in humans.

The eyes of Axolotls are lidless – they can't blink their eyes.

Note that the overall shape of the bodies of males and females are also quite different. The females have wider bodies than the males – as the females need space to carry their eggs when they get pregnant. This is also the reason why females are typically bigger and heavier than the males.

Remember their gills? They actually have external and internal gills. They have three pairs of external gills that are located behind their heads – so, there are three on the left side and three on the right side.

Underneath their external gills are gill slits. These gill slits connect with the internal gills of the Axolotl.

Males VS females

Male axolotls usually have a slightly longer tail than females. Males also always have a swollen cloacal region, even outside the breeding season. This is not the case with females. However, the gender can only be determined after about one year, or when they are about twenty centimetres big.

A male reaches reproductive maturity at about one to two years. Females usually become reproductively mature earlier and can reproduce after about one year.

As in many other species, the male performs a "mating dance" at breeding time to "seduce" the female. During the mating dance, the male has his long tail towered, wags it back and forth and also nudges the female to encourage her to mate.

The females usually produce around 80 to 700 eggs and lay them on water plants. This happens about every two months. The eggs are not always actually fertilised. When fertilised, a small axolotl develops inside the egg - this process is called *paedogenesis*. Usually, axolotls hatch after about 10 to 20 days. They then feed on the yolk for a few more days.

The babies are already born independently and can move around without any problems. After five weeks they measure about five to six centimetres.

As axolotls are not solitary animals, they should be kept at least in pairs.

Of course, if you have only males, egg-laying will never occur. Some owners prefer this.

Axolotls living together should be about the same size so that the larger axolotl does not - voluntarily or involuntarily - attack or try to swallow the smaller axolotl. Smaller axolotls are easily eaten by larger ones. As a worst-case scenario, the smaller axolotl may be even too big to eat and may get stuck in the mouth of the larger axolotl. Both animals can die from this! It is therefore very important that the animals are approximately the same size.

Types and colours

The axolotl types can be roughly divided into four categories:

1. Albinos

2. Coppers

3. Whites (Leucistic)

4. Wildlings (Melanoid)

Albinos are white or yellowish and can also be somewhat shiny or shimmery. Their eggs are white. Due to an enzyme defect, albinos do not have melanin, which would otherwise ca use a darker colouration. The enzyme that albinos do not have is tyrosinase (amino acid = tyrosine).

Coppers come in many colours, such as yellow, brown, white, copper. They can also shimmer a little. Their eggs are beige/light brown. In contrast to the albinos, they do have tyrosine or tyrosinase, but they do not produce melanin either, only phaeomelanin. Phaeomelanin is a pigment which, together with eumelanin (also a pigment), determines the colour of t he skin.

Wildlings (melanonids) are usually black and/or brown. Sometimes a yellowish colouration occurs. Their eggs are also dark.

The colour of the eggs does not (always) indicate what the larva will look like later. The colour of the eggs depends on the colour of the mother. However, the colouration of the emerging larva does not depend on the mother alone, but on both parents.

Unfortunately, in some countries axolotls have been dyed or given colour pigments so that they "shine" in numerous bright colours (red, pink, green etc.). It is not advisable to buy a dyed animal.

Like all amphibians, the "normal" axolotl has three kinds of cells responsible for the pigmentation of the skin and eyes, the chromatophores.

The melanophores carry pigments (melanin and others) responsible for black and brown colors The xanthophores carry the yellow color The iridiophores are pigmentary cells that reflect light.

There were already animals in the wild that showed a different color (or lack of color) from the usual wild type: pink axolotls were among the animals brought back to the Museum in 1863, which are largely (but not exclusively, as is sometimes said) the ancestors of our domestic axolotls. It is also known that the diversification of colors and coats is one of the first consequences of the domestication of a species.

The main genetic mutations determining the appearance of forms of different color are albinism, xanthism.

Albinism corresponds to the absence of black pigment, or to a very reduced production of them by the organism. In true albinism, the total absence of pigment, the eyes are pink. Albinism is genetically associated with many malformations (especially the absence of eyes) in some species, which makes the embryos not viable, and this i s probably also the case in the axolotl. Where possible, albino juveniles are more fragile and vulnerable than juveniles with wild-type coloration and suffer higher mortality rates at all stages of development. They are more easily spotted by predators and are less efficient at foraging due to their poor eyesight. They are also more susceptible to cellular dysfunction and more susceptible to disease. This is why a "marriage" likely to produce, in the same egg-laying, pigmented larvae and albinos in proportions predictable from the genetic probabilities usually results in an effective number of albinos lower than expected.

The pink axolotls common in captivity (w hich are in fact white, it is their red blood that makes them look pink) are not albinos in the strict sense, but partial albinos. The scientific term is leucistic. Their eyes are pigmented and they can show localized traces of pigmentation, usually on the gill racks and on the top of the head.

The full albino axolotl exists in captivity, however, it is the result of genetic manipulation in the laboratory. It is a hybrid, more exactly a "chimera". The American biologist Humphrey succeeded in the 1960s in transferring in vitro the gene of albinism taken from a female of Ambystoma tigrinum into the genome of an axolotl. The eggs developed into adult axolotl and their offspring proved to be stable in their characters and fertile, even after crossing with ordinary axolotls, although the breeding is more delicate. The neoteny is preserved. There are two forms of this type, the full albino and the "gold" axolotl. The first one is completely depigmented. The axolotl "gold" is completely devoid of melanophores, with red eyes. However, the xanthofores are present in attenuated form, as the melanophores were present in attenuated form in the leucistic axolotl and the animal has a more or less yellow coloration.

The leucistic mutation and albinism are called recessive. That is to say that their effects are manifested on the color of the animal - we say that the gene is expressed - only if the mutant gene is present TWICE on the allele formed by the two chromosomes (homozygous), therefore if it was transmitted by the father AND by the mother. When it is present only once (heterozygous), the animal is genetically carrier without affecting its appearance (phenotype). It can always be transmitted to its descendants. It follows that:

- Two mutant animals that are both pink, gold or albino only give mutant offspring: all pink, gold or albino, depending on the gene of the parents (homozygous mutants).
- Two animals without the mutant gene give only offspring resembling the parents (pigmented), not carriers (homozygous pigmented).
- Two parents of which one is a carrier of the gene and the other one is not, give only first generation offspring resembling the parents, pigmented, of which a part (50%) remain carriers of the gene (heterozygous mutants).
- Two parents who carry the gene without showing it give first generation offspring: for a quarter mutant (homozygous), for another quarter pigmented, non-carriers, and for half pigmented but carrying the gene (heterozygous mutants).

This is the simplest case because it involves only two cases, the presence or absence of mutation on a single gene, for a single color. Insofar as we can have several colors in play (melanophores and xanthophores), with variants of these, where some colorations involve several genes, and where a given genetic profile can lead to animals externally quite different from each other, for example, depending on the degree of pigmentation expressed in a leucistic axolotl, there are other forms of colorations. Hobbyists continue to select these and try to develop new ones, without genetic manipulation, by choosing the breeding stock in such a way as to strengthen this or that trait present in the parents.

In the end, we distinguish the following types, some of which are quite rare:

- Wild type (grey-black pigmented, melanophores, xanthophores and Iridiophores)
- Copper: Copper is a pigmented form with another color than the wild type, brown rather than gray, i.e. brown spots on a copper background; It is a rather rare color whose genetics is not completely elucidated. We do not know if it is a spontaneous color already present in the genetic heritage of the wild axolotl, a form that appeared spontaneously in captivity (mutation) and then retained by selection, or a hybridization. The reproduction of the "copper" is often

laborious, all the eggs are not viable, clearly because of genetic problems. This may be due to hybrid inheritance or to excessive inbreeding as a result of inbreeding to fix the strain. It would be necessary to enlarge the gene pool by introducing wild type animals.

- Leucistics (melanophore inhibition). Animals that have visible melanophores, although inhibited overall, are said to be harlequin. A harlequin is genetically leucistic (homozygous for partial albinism), but it can carry the genes for other colors.

- Gold (inhibition of xanthophores) White albino: no pigment, the animal is both albino (without melanophores) and axanthic (without xanthophores)

- Melanic : pigmented animals but without iriodophores, which means for example that the eyes are without a golden circle around the pupil and that their coat tends to be more plain. They can exist in different colors and their gradations: Black, Grey, White, Gold, Albino or Copper.

Endangered Species

There have always been a few natural threats to the Axolotl's survival, including predatory birds like herons.

More recently, however, Axolotls have begun to suffer from the introduction of large numbers of fish, like carp, into their lake habitat. These fish compete with Axolotls for food and also eat Axolotl eggs.

Herons are natural predators of the Axolotl. The Axolotl population has decreased as a result.

Axolotls are also popular as pets and as food. Roasted Axolotl is a festive treat in Mexico.

All these factors have had the effect of further shrinking Axolotl numbers in the wild. They are now considered a critically endangered species – a species likely to become extinct.

Their popularity as pets, however, means that despite the challenges they face in the wild, Axolotls continue to thrive. Even if they can no longer be found in their natural habitat one day, we will still be able to enjoy them in captivity for many years to come.

Chapter 2: Getting the axolotls

Buying axolotls

When buying a pet, many people first turn to the traditional and established pet store. Unfortunately, however, pet stores often give bad advice. This is not only the case with axolotls, but also with other popular pets like rabbits, hamsters, etc.

Also, pet stores often sell axolotls that should not be given as gifts. Some animals are injured or sick and are sold anyway. In addition, up-to-date BD testing (see "Common Diseases") is often not done at the pet store and so pathogens can easily be picked up. Also, pet stores often sell axolotls that are too small and not yet ready to be given away. Axolotls should be at least ten inches in size when they are delivered. In most cases, this size is reached at the age of three or four months.

It is therefore a better alternative to buy axolotls from a reputable breeder or get them second hand. The animals should of course look healthy and have no injuries. In addition, an up-to-date BD test should be submitted at the time of delivery to make sure you don't bring this deadly disease into your home.

A reputable breeder will prepare the animals for transport. It is best to bring a secure food box with you to pick up the animals, which can be used later as a quarantine box. The breeder will pack the axolotls in a suitable transport bag. The bag should be one-third full of cold water and two-thirds full of air. These bags should be carefully placed in the transport box. The exact procedure should be discussed prior to harvesting.

First of all, it is necessary to acquire healthy animals. To do this, look especially at the skin and gills. The skin must be normally colored, free of wounds, veils, spots foreign to the normal coloration of the animal, fungal growths, lumps and tumors etc... The gills must be in the required number, free, long and, with blood capillaries well present and well irrigated, well red in depigmented animals. The eyes should not be cloudy or whitish, a sign of bacterial infection or excess fat in the diet. Axolotls should be of normal weight, neither emaciated (the body is much smaller than the head) nor bloated. We will also make sure that the cloaca does not present any abnormal growths. Refusal to eat is a symptom of disease. So is floating on its back.

If the axolotl is to be transported in the summer, it is best to carry cold packs or a large cooler bag. This ensures that the water does not get (too) hot during transport.

Cost Of Getting One

Continuously obtain a creature from a trustworthy raiser or salvage gathering. It's best not to purchase an axolotl through the web or an arranged promotion except if you've spoken straightforwardly with the dealer, and they're ready to give you sufficient data on the creature. On the off chance that they can't give you careful documentation on its cause and wellbeing history, that is a warning. It's likewise ideal to talk with individuals who have procured creatures from that dealer to reveal any worries. Also, a neighborhood extraordinary veterinarian regularly can guide you to a decent raiser or salvage.

Hope to pay somewhere in the range of $20 and $70 by and large. Creatures with more uncommon shading, for example, copper, will in general cost more. A sound axolotl will be dynamic, and it may acknowledge food in the event that you offer it. Its skin shouldn't be flaky, and its body ought to be fairly full (instead of underweight), however it shouldn't have any unusual expanding.

Capturing and transporting the axolotl

To avoid damaging the protective mucus of the axolotl's skin, it is preferable to capture it with a container rather than with a net. If you have to handle it, you must wet your hands beforehand. For transportation, the animal must be able to access the atmospheric air, so never in a container filled to the brim. The buckets (up to 18 liters) used by fishermen to transport live fish, preferably with a flat bottom, are suitable for long term transport. These buckets contain a removable plastic mesh cage that can also be used to capture animals. The water remains aerated. A water height of 5 cm is sufficient. To avoid the production of excrement and regurgitation due to stress, the animals should not be fed for 48 hours before transport.

Quarantine

Before an axolotl moves into its new home, it should first be kept in quarantine. The quarantine period is usually four to six weeks and is completed individually. Several axolotls should not be placed in the same quarantine box.

One food-safe plastic box per axolotl is used for quarantine. Of course, an axolotl can also be placed in another, empty tank if one is left. It is important that the quarantine home is square. Round boxes or other containers are not suitable, as an axolotl orients itself to the walls (the so-called *lateral line system*).

The boxes should be able to hold about 10 to 15 litres of water (*about 2.7 to 4 gallons*). The lid does not need any holes, as axolotls absorb their oxygen through the water. The colder the water (ideally 12°C to 17°C / 53°F to 63°F), the higher the oxygen content of the water.

Quarantine boxes are particularly important in the following cases:

1. A completely new tank is set up in which no axolotls live yet. This must first be brought into a healthy equilibrium (see 'cycling phase'). In the meantime, the axolotls can spend their quarantine phase in the boxes described above.

2. A new axolotl is to be integrated into the group. Example: Only one axolotl was previously kept in solitary confinement (not species-

appropriate!) or a new friend is to enrich the existing group. Regardless of whether this axolotl comes from a breeder or a previous owner: the quarantine period should be completed so that the new axolotl does not introduce any pathogens and can first recover from the stress before it moves into its new home.

3. A slight illness has been detected, for example a fungal infection or a slight bite, and the affected axolotl should first recover, receive a salt bath or similar. Fungal infections should not be confused with more serious diseases.

Socialisation

Usually, axolotls are offered dead food - dead worms, small pieces of fish, pellets with a large proportion of animal protein and the like. However, some keepers also want to offer their axolotls living food. This is often not recommended, for good reasons.

The only creatures that can possibly be kept together with axolotls are endler's guppies, dwarf shrimps (**neocaridina**), bubble snails, post horn snails, cardinal fish and zebra danios. Please note, however, that these animals are eaten by the axolotls in 99% of cases!

All other animal species must never be kept together with axolotls! There are several reasons for this. Firstly, many animals are simply too big to eat, but this does not stop the axolotls from trying. There are often "accidents" where an axolotl tries to eat a large fish and it gets stuck in its mouth. This is not good for either the axolotl or the fish and can be fatal!

It is particularly bad when an axolotl tries to eat a catfish, for example. For one thing, a catfish is too big to be eaten anyway and will get stuck in its mouth. However, it also has barbs on the end of its head, which make removing the fish very dangerous! The barbs of the catfish hook into the mouth of the axolotl. Sometimes a skilled vet can cut it out, sometimes both animals die trying. This is just one example of many.

There are also fish species (even small ones which "look harmless") that nibble or suck on the axolotl. The gill branches or even the tail is particularly often injured in the process!

It is therefore safest and most advisable to keep axolotls only with other axolotls! Please do not confuse axolotls with Andersonis and do not keep them together either! Due to the similar appearance, the layman can sometimes confuse an axolotl with an Andersoni. Andersoni only occur in the pattern/colours of the wild animal. With a size of 18 to 20 centimetres, Andersoni remain smaller than Axolotls. There is a risk that an adult axolotl will try to eat an Andersoni. In addition, Andersoni are diurnal, while Axolotls are nocturnal. Andersoni are still much more active than axolotls and often more aggressive.

Chapter 3: Axolotl Feeding

Axolotl are carnivorous, that is, meat-eating. In the wild they can survive for up to 15 years on a diet of small prey such as worms, crustaceans, molluscs, insects and small fish.

Axolotls are carnivorous. Axolotls locate food by smell, and will "snap" at any potential meal, sucking th e food into their stomachs with strong, vacuum force. Cool!

However, they do also have small teeth which can be used to grasp food before swallowing it completely.

Feeding the axolotl

In principle, the capture of food is a reflex stimulated by the detection of the prey's movement. After a certain age, after the different larval stages, it is nevertheless possible to accustom the animal to take inert foods provided that they are recognizable by taste or smell and that their size interests the animal. Food that is too small is disdained. This said, the axolotl is not fussy: it accepts live, thawed, industrial foods which it prefers to take on the bottom.

Some amateurs avoid marine foods (thawed pieces of sea fish, such as smelts, mussels, shrimps or pieces of pink shrimps, krill etc...) because they are likely to contain a significant amount of iodine. Iodine interferes with the thyroid gland and we have seen that the particular functioning of this one was responsible for the neoteny of the axolotl. We personally do not see any inconvenience in distributing mussel mantle to adult axolotls, the fleshy part located on both sides of the mussel which is easily detached after boiling a pre-cooked frozen mussel which is left to soak a little to rinse it. These pieces are about the right size for an adult axolotl, with two pieces of mantle per meal. Frozen or raw sea fish may contain a substance (thiaminase) that is detrimental to the metabolism of vitamins over time. Thawed fillet pieces of freshwater fish (trout) are preferable. In general we share a widespread prevention against small pieces of beef (cooked or raw) which are poorly digested by amphibians and may contain thyroid remnants. If necessary, beef heart, without any trace of blood, and poultry liver, occasionally and in small quantities, for example to "restock" a slimmed down animal, are preferred.

This leads to a preference for live foods and commercial foods.

Among the commercial feeds, there are special "pellets" (sticks) for axolotls. They are essential during the growth of the larvae, but their composition is often too much vegetable matter (spirulina) and it is difficult to find pellets big enough to interest adult axolotls. Pellets for bottom fish (fresh water) can be tempted, provided they are not predominantly vegetal either. Floating chaff-type foods should be avoided. No more dry food should be fed than the animals can consume in 5 minutes without leaving anything behind.

Live food should be clean - from unpolluted environments - and sink to the bottom. Most earthworms (like earthworms, eisenia, eiseniella, dendrob(a)ena etc...) are appreciated. They are easy to find in fish stores, in the aquarium trade or in home compost. They keep well in the refrigerator's vegetable bin. One or two worms make a meal for an adult axolotl.

Frozen fish food (bloodworms) are not very interesting, and even risky: some aquatic parasites can survive freezing, and the worms can come from soiled environments (sewage ponds). Mealworms are accepted, although they are difficult to digest because of their chitinous exoskeleton. Freshly molted worms, recognizable by their white color, are preferred. Sowbugs are small, difficult to detect, but can be appreciated from time to time for the calcium phosphate and limestone they contain in their shells.

In general, a certain diversity in the food offered must be observed to avoid nutritional deficiencies. An alternative food will be proposed every two or three weeks.

Axolotls are nocturnal hunters who lie in wait. They usually remain in one place and wait there for their prey. They do not actively search for food but wait for it at a fixed point and are therefore often very patient. Their food includes almost everything they can overpower, for example insects and their larvae, worms, small fish and their eggs and small crustaceans. This can also be offered to a domesticated axolotl relatively easily and without much effort.

Axolotls either catch their prey as it swims by or they pick up their food from the bottom.

Axolotls are carnivores (meat eaters). They cannot digest plant food efficiently and are therefore dependent on animal food. This is also the case, for example, with the generally popular domestic cat. It is best to offer the axolotls fresh food: small pieces of fish, worms (e.g., earthworms such as giant red worms/Dendrobena), small snails, small crustaceans and the like. Long worms are best cut up once before feeding.

However, it is not recommended to collect worms and other animals outside. It is possible for animals from the wild to introduce pathogens into the tank!

In addition, pellets are offered on the market which have a high vegetable content. As axolotls are strict carnivores, these should not be used. Axolotls cannot utilise these vegetable components anyway. Therefore, pellets should consist of at least 60% animal protein!

It is also possible to feed frozen fish from the supermarket. Of course, the frozen fish should not be seasoned. It should also not have any bones. If bones are present, they must be removed before feeding. Fish should not be fed in too large pieces - therefore it should be cut into bite-sized pieces beforehand. For example, the pieces of fish can be 1 cm x 3 cm (*for example 0.4 inches x 1.2 inches*). Ideally, each axolotl should be fed five to six pieces per feeding. If worms, small crustaceans, pellets or small snails are also fed, the quantities should be adjusted individually.

Suitable fish species include trout, pike, pikeperch, eel, sturgeon, carp or perch. If possible, however, freshwater fish should be preferred in order to avoid the administration of iodine.

The meat of mammals such as chicken should not be fed. On the one hand, this is unnatural, as axolotls do not feed on chicken or similar meat in nature. Secondly, this type of meat is more difficult for axolotls to digest. Seaweed is also not suitable, as it naturally contains a high proportion of iodine. Iodine could cause axolotls to go into metamorphosis, which must be prevented.

Food remains can be easily removed with the help of food tongs.

Pellets, industrial dried food

Fresh food is the best choice for feeding axolotls, as this is what they naturally feed on in the wild. Frozen food can partly replace fresh food or at least complement it well. Pellets or industrially produced dry food are not usually necessary, as such food does not correspond to the natural diet of axolotls. However, there are cases in which pellets must be used or in which pellets can be offered as a supplement.

If you want to feed pellets, pay close attention to the composition of the ingredients. The qualitative differences between the individual products are sometimes huge. There are pellets on the market that contain only 20-30% fish. These are not at all suitable for an axolotl, as the axolotl is a carnivore. For example, there are pellets on the market with a raw protein content of over 50% - these are well suited as supplementary food.

Unhealthy additives should also not be found in the pellets. Many industrial animal feeds, for example, are enriched with "vegetable by-products" to keep costs down. This is a nicer word for "waste". Vegetable by-products are generated during the production of other products. To prevent them from going to waste, they are added to animal feed, for example. This is also often the case with rodent food. The same applies to "animal by-products".

Vegetable by-products offer no added value for axolotls. They are neither healthy nor species-appropriate, as axolotls are of course not herbivores or omnivores. These ingredients are excreted again anyway without being used.

Nevertheless, it must be mentioned that pellets entirely without any plant ingredients are not offered at this time. A small component of plant ingredients is necessary to hold the individual components of the pellets together, as they act like a "glue".

These ingredients are small individual particles that slowly dissolve in the water if the pellets are not eaten by the axolotls. If pellets are offered, they must be eaten quickly by the animals, otherwise there is a risk of extreme contamination of the aquarium water. If individual pellets are not eaten, they should be removed from the aquarium within an hour.

Pellets should never be the sole food of the axolotl, as this would simply be too one-sided and unhealthy. If pellets are used, they should make up a maximum of one fifth or one quarter of the total food quantity. Otherwise, there is a risk of nutrient deficiency in the animals. The animal components of the pellets should make up at least 45%.

Food from Nature – Yes or No?

There are some axolotl keepers who look for food for their animals in the wild. This primarily involves worms such as earthworms.

Whether this is recommendable is highly controversial. I personally do not recommend it. On the one hand, axolotls don't eat very much and not very often - so it actually makes little or no difference to your finances whether you collect food for the axolotls in the wild or not. The financial aspects are negligible, also because worms can be grown / bred quite easily at home. Many axolotl keepers breed their own earthworms in a box or bucket, for example. This minimises the risk of pathogens or harmful substances.

In addition, collected food from the wild offers no more value compared to purchased or home-bred fresh worms. The little animals from the wild are not better or more nutritious than the purchased feed, as long as they are alive / fresh.

Live food can introduce parasites and other pathogens into the axolotl's aquarium. With a carnivorous animal like the axolotl, the risk of this is always higher than with an herbivorous animal like guinea pigs, rabbits, *etc.* - because parasites often use worms and insects as intermediate hosts on which they nest for a while. If food containing pathogens is introduced into the axolotl aquarium, these pathogens and parasites will quite quickly pass on to the axolotl group and use them as hosts.

Of course, this is also possible if the food is bought or home-bred. As a rule, such a risk cannot be ruled out. However, the risk is higher if the food is collected in the wild.

Other toxins could also be accidentally introduced into the aquarium if the feed is obtained from the wild. Here, of course, it depends in which areas and on which land is collected. Pesticides, rat poisons and other harmful substances are a real risk that can be avoided.

Finally, some precautions should be observed when distributing food.

Do not overfeed Obesity, with fatal consequences, threatens amphibians and aquarium fish. In addition, uneaten food and excess excrement are pollution factors. One or two pieces of mussel mantle, one or two earthworms, every two or three days are enough food for an adult axolotl. Feeding should be stopped when the temperature is low or during hot spells. It is also preferable to let the adult axolotls fast for one or two weeks (or even more) rather than to see them force-feed by an inexperienced hand. You can also anticipate an absence by increasing the frequency of meals a little before it.

The axolotl is a bit laborious in its search for food. When several animals live together, there is always the possibility that some do not arrive in time, that some eat too much and others do not.

In the wild, axolotls feed on snails, worms, shellfish, little fish, and little creatures of land and water. In bondage, they can be taken care of an assortment of saline solution shrimp, little segments of meat or liver, night crawlers, bloodworms, tubifex worms, other solidified fish nourishments, and business fish pellets. Try not to take care of any worms or fish you got yourself, as they can convey parasites. All in all, no nutrient or mineral enhancements are fundamental.

Counsel your veterinarian with respect to the measure of food to offer, just as how frequently to take care of your axolotl, as this differs relying upon age and size. When all is said in done, numerous grown-ups take a few feedings for each week. Probably the best strategy to take care of is by holding the food in round-nosed forceps in the tank close to the creature. You additionally can just drop the food in the water as near the axolotl as could be expected under the circumstances. In the event that your axolotl isn't keen on eating much during the day, have a go at taking care of it at night when it's regularly more dynamic. Expel any uneaten food from the tank each day to keep the water clean.

Feeding Frequency

Most axolotls do not need to be fed daily; the larger the animal gets, the less often it needs food. Therefore, it is usually no problem to go away for the weekend and leave the animals alone for a few days. However, in the case of a longer absence, holiday care should be organised.

Adult axolotls can even fast for about ten days without suffering any damage. However, with a longer fasting period, there is a risk that axolotls will turn on each other and, in a worst-case scenario, injure or mutilate each other.

The feeding rhythm can be very individual, so always keep a close eye on the animals. If an axolotl gains a lot of weight, the time between two feedings should be extended. Overfeeding the animals should be taken very seriously and can often even lead to death. Domesticated axolotls often do not select according to their natural instinct but eat whatever the owner makes available to them. Obesity can lead to diseases of the gastrointestinal tract, fatty liver and other feeding-related diseases.

As a general rule of thumb ...

... with a body size of up to 12 centimetres (*up to 4.7 inches*), axolotls should be fed every day.

... with a body size of up to about 16 centimetres (*up to about 6.3 inches*), they can be fed every two days.

... with a body size of up to about 18 centimetres (*up to about 7 inches*), they can be fed every three days.

... with a body size of more than 18 centimetres (*more than 7 inches*), they can be fed once or twice a week - most owners feed their adult animals only once a week.

To reiterate: These are only guidelines. The animals should always be closely observed to determine whether a normal body weight is maintained or whether the animal may be slowly tending towards obesity (fatty liver and other organs!). Accordingly, the fasting period can be extended or shortened.

Fasting periods of one to two weeks are usually considered problem-free (for adult axolotls). Therefore, the owners can go away for the weekend or take a short holiday without necessarily having someone come home to feed the animals. When the fasting phase is too long is quite controversial in the axolotl community. However, the general principle is that two weeks without food should not be exceeded, as otherwise the animals could start attacking each other and maiming or injuring themselves. If you are going on a two-or three-week holiday, it is a good idea to have someone come home once or twice during this time to feed the animals. After all, this does not take up a lot of time.

The Digestive Tract of the Axolotl

Axolotls have a rather flat and rounded head. When the mouth is closed, it might appear quite small - but appearances are deceptive, because the mouth can be opened wide and is quite big.

The mouths of axolotls are underslung (inferior). The underslung mouth is typical for animals that mainly look for their prey at the bottom of the water and usually stay there. With an underslung mouth, the lower jaw is shorter than the upper jaw and the opening of the mouth thus points downwards.

When not feeding, the axolotl's mouth is closed. However, if the axolotl keeps its mouth permanently open, something is usually wrong. The axolotl may have ingested too large a chunk of food, its stomach may be overloaded, or it may be infested with parasites such as nematodes. If the mouth is permanently open, the cause should definitely be identified.

As axolotls are pure carnivores, their digestive tract is dependent on animal food. Only this type of food can be completely digested and utilised by the animal. Vegetable food should therefore be avoided. This offers the axolotl no added value and is simply excreted without being utilised.

Axolotls can vomit. Since domesticated axolotls do not regulate their food intake themselves but eat almost everything that is offered to them by humans, the stomach can become overloaded, causing vomiting. Feeding too quickly or too frequently can also cause vomiting. In this case, the amount of food should be reduced and the intervals between two feedings can be extended.

If an axolotl vomits, this can also be due to spoiled food. In any case, it should be checked whether the food is still fresh or, if in doubt, it should be disposed of.

A bacterial disease or parasite infestation can also trigger vomiting. If the axolotl has not ingested any spoiled food and the amount of food was definitely not too large, it should be examined whether the axolotl is possibly ill.

In addition, axolotls can also fall ill with diarrhoea, their faeces can be covered with mucus or blood can be found in the faeces. Such cases are almost always due to diseases such as infections, parasites, fungal diseases and the like. But swallowing stones can also cause blood in the faeces and, of course, constipation.

How often axolotls defecate depends mainly on their age. Young ones need food much more often than adult axolotls, so the young also defecate more frequently. It is normal for very young axolotls (until they are about ten centimetres (four inches) big) to defecate every day. However, these animals are also fed daily. This is no longer the case with adult axolotls. Since adult axolotls eat less frequently, it is normal for them to defecate only about once or twice a week.

Occasionally, axolotls may swallow too much air. This happens quite often, especially with young axolotls. They then float close to the water surface and usually paddle around helplessly. This happens because there is too much air in the digestive tract and is usually caused by the axolotl being too greedy when taking in food and accidentally taking in too much air. Usually, this condition normalises itself and the axolotl lets the excess air escape. However, if it does not manage to do this, the axolotl may need to be examined by a specialist vet who has experience with amphibians. Normally this is quite harmless and will quickly disappear. However, if it happens frequently, it should be checked whether the animal is getting enough food and whether the food is easily accessible.

The digestive tract of an axolotl is that of a carnivore. Therefore, the intestine only absorbs and utilises nutrients from animal food. Vegetable food components are not or hardly utilised. They pass through the intestine but are largely excreted unused. A permanent feeding of plant food can also cause the intestine of an axolotl to become diseased, as it is simply not designed to have to process food other than animal food.

Axolotls have a cloaca - this is the common outlet of both the intestine and urinary bladder and the genital organ. Male axolotls have a larger cloaca than females. The cloaca of a male appears swollen (even if it is not actually swollen) and can therefore be easily identified with the naked eye.

The cloaca is part of the animal's rectum; not only excrement is excreted here, but also the sperm of the males and the eggs of the females.

Natural Foraging

Axolotls are nocturnal lurking hunters. Lurking hunters include carnivorous animals, which usually do not actively hunt and pursue their prey but remain in a certain place and wait there (patiently) for their prey. When the prey - for example, a small fish - swims past the axolotl, it attacks and grabs the prey animal.

To do this, the axolotl makes use of its electro and pressure receptors. For example, it has ampullary organs (ampullary receptors) and uses the lateral line system. This enables the axolotl to recognise or locate its prey.

When an animal moves in the water, this creates pressure fluctuations. The axolotl can perceive these with the help of its lateral line system.

Ampullary organs, on the other hand, perceive electro impulses that are generated by muscle activity. This also represents a stimulus for the axolotl and causes it to feed.

Axolotls are farsighted and therefore do not rely on their sense of sight when searching for food, but on the triggered stimuli described above to perceive food and to snatch it. Furthermore, the sense of smell is well developed and supports the animals in their search for food - especially when foraging on the ground.

Axolotls exercise a great deal of patience when lurking and sometimes remain in the same spot for hours in the wild. While a prey animal in an "active hunt" (chase) is aware that it is being pursued and accordingly tries to flee, the prey of the lurking hunters is usually surprised and does not expect an attack. Accordingly, lurking hunters have to expend much less energy than chasers, but of course they need a lot of patience and attention. Since axolotls need comparatively little food, this type of hunting is ideal for them.

They are "suction snappers". This means that they suck in their food suddenly and unexpectedly before the prey can flee. However, this is also practised when the prey is already dead or simply lying still.

However, axolotls do not only wait for prey to swim by, but also often collect their food from the bottom of the water. In the process, it can happen that the animals also suck in some substrate and this gets into their digestive tract. For this reason, stones that are too large should not be used as substrate. In some countries, natural, rounded pebbles of a maximum size of three millimetres are used, in other countries, substrate is not used at all.

Fine sand is a good compromise, because it is better for the locomotion of the axolotl and for the bacterial balance in the aquarium if the bottom is covered. However, fine sand grains are of course very small, so that occasional swallowing does not pose a danger and does not cause blockages, as could be the case with larger stones.

Chapter 4: Axolotl Aquarium

Setting up Your Axolotl Tank

At any rate a 15-to 20-gallon fish tank is suggested for axolotls. Ensure the tank has a protected top, as it's normal for these creatures to attempt to leap out of their nook. A land zone is superfluous in the tank for these completely amphibian creatures. At the very least, the water profundity ought to be somewhat more than the length of your axolotl. Be that as it may, including additional profundity will help with water quality and give your creature more space to move.

Axolotls are relatively easy to care for and feel comfortable in a species-appropriate tank. Two to three axo lotls should have at least

0.5 square metres (*5 square feet*) of space available. For example, a 200-litre tank measuring 100 cm x 50 cm x 40 cm (*roughly 40 inches x 20 inches x 15 inches*) is great. The height of the tank is not too relevant; more important is the floor space of at least half a square metre (*at least five square feet*). Of course, the home may also be larger; the more space, the better!

The axolotl's home should be angular - a rounded shape should be avoided, otherwise the animals will not be able to orientate themselves well. It should also be made of glass; plastic is rather unsuitable. The tank does not need a cover. It is even better if the tank is open, as these do not heat up as much as closed tanks. An open tank is also easier to handle when cleaning and feeding. If cats or similar are also kept at the same time, the tank can also be protected with a sturdy grid lid so that other animals are kept away from the axolotls.

Get the tank in a cool room far from brilliant daylight with the water temperature somewhere in the range of 57 and 68 degrees Fahrenheit (14 and 20 degrees Celsius); don't permit it to get over 75 degrees Fahrenheit (24 degrees Celsius). No unique lighting is required for axolotls (in contrast to numerous reptiles). Actually, a dull concealing spot, for example, a vase laid on its side or an aquarium mansion, is frequently valued.

A few proprietors select to leave the base of the tank exposed, however others accept this may pressure the axolotl on the off chance that it can't get a traction on the smooth base. In the event that rock is utilized on the base, it must be coarse rock that is greater than the axolotl's head. Fine rock may be ingested and cause a deterrent.

Faucet water treated with an aquarium water conditioner that expels chlorine and chloramines is fine for axolotls. Never use refined water, and ensure the pH of the water stays somewhere in the range of 6.5 and 7.5. (You can discover a water test pack to check all things considered pet stores.) Most proprietors discover a sifted aquarium is simpler to keep up on the grounds that unfiltered water needs visit changing to evacuate squander.

Axolotl care is a bit different than that of the fishbowl or aquarium fish you might be used to. We've put together a bookshelf that contains everything you feel necessity for to be aware about setting up an Axolotl container and caring for these amazing creatures.

Axolotls are relatively easy to care for and are comfortable in an aquarium that is suitable for the species. Two or three axolotls should have at least 0.5 square meters of space available. For example, a 200-gallon aquarium measuring 100 cm x 50 cm x 40 cm (about 40 inches x 20 inches x 15 inches) is fine. The height of the aquarium is not too important; more important is the floor space of at least half a square meter (at least five square feet). Of course, the aquarium can also be larger; the more space, the better!

The axolotl aquarium should be angular - a rounded shape should be avoided, otherwise the animals will not be able to orient themselves well. It should also be made of glass; plastic is rather unsuitable. The aquarium does not need a lid. It's even better if the aquarium is open, because it doesn't get as hot as closed tanks. An open aquarium is also easier to handle when cleaning and feeding. If you are also keeping cats or the like at the same time, the aquarium can also be protected with a sturdy grid lid so that other animals are kept away from the axolotl.

Ten aquatic plants that are well suited to the axolotl aquarium:

1. Elodea / Water Plague

2. Microsorum pteropus

3. Java moss (Vesicularia dubyana)

4. Spathiphyllum

5. Anubias

6. Cabomba

7. Ceratophyllum demersum

8. Saururus

9. Rorippa aquatica

10. Echinodorus

Excessive hygiene can do more harm than good. Although excess nitrate and other germs should be removed during cleaning, the bottom and filter should not be cleaned too meticulously. More on this later!

The filter should ideally be an external filter suitable for the size of the aquarium. Plastic internal filters are less suitable. The pipe should be just below the water surface so that the surface moves, but axolotls don't pay too much attention to this - they don't like currents, preferring still or stagnant water. Starter bacteria are not necessary. The important bacteria form during the cycling phase, and a balance is achieved in the aquarium naturally. However, a bottom filter is also possible.

In addition, it is advisable to place the aquarium on a stable surface. It should be easy for people to reach so that cleaning and water changes can be done comfortably. The furniture on which the aquarium is to stand should be able to support a load of at least 200 kilograms (at least 440 pounds).

The Axolotls should have a few hiding places available. These should of course be disinfected in advance - as should all accessories - so that no pathogens are introduced into the house. Axolotls also use plants to hide, but some caves etc. should be available. At least one hiding place per axolotl should be provided so that axolotls do not fight over hiding places. Wood is not suitable. Coconut caves are popular because of their appearance, but they are also not suitable. Accessories should be made of stone or clay. It is a good idea to bake them in the oven before use to kill pathogens. Ideally, baking accessories should be baked at 100°C for about one to two hours. Pipes and caves are usually especially popular.

Cycling Your Fishbowl or aquarium

Fill up your fishbowl or aquarium and turn on equipment as well as the strainer and heater. If you want, you is able as well put all decorations (discussed below) in their respective areas. After this it's period to start the cycle!

Cycling your fishbowl or aquarium means you provide it period to accumulate beneficial bacteria in the strainer and substratum. These bacteria are the just thing making the container safe for your future Axolotls, so it pays to put few effort into this.

To cycle an fishbowl or aquarium, you kickstart the process by adding ammonia. We choose applying unscented household ammonia as it's not hard to dose and doesn't make a mess.

Water

Most axolotl breeders agree that water temperature is probably the most important criterion for good maintenance. As mentioned above, axolotls need fresh, oxygen-rich water. Clean, high quality tap water is usually sufficient. Fertilizer and starter bacteria are not necessary. Water conditioners can also be dispensed with.

The optimal water temperature is between about 10°C and 20°C (50°F to 68°F). In an emergency, the temperature can go as low as 72°F (22°C), but this should be a big exception. If the water temperature is too high, axolotls feel extremely stressed and are more susceptible to disease. Especially in the summer months, temperature can become an issue. If the temperature is too high, the risk of fungal diseases is also greatly increased. However, if the temperature drops too low and is below 10°C (less than 50°F), the axolotl's metabolism is slowed, and this can be very hard on digestion.

To keep the water temperature within the optimal limits (6-20°), choose a room that is not subject to overheating in summer and a location away from the heater. It is also important not to expose the aquarium to direct sunlight (window) in order not to increase the temperature rise and to prevent the proliferation of algae on the walls. Unlike temperate zone amphibians, the axolotl does not necessarily need an annual temperature cycle. It can reproduce without having undergone a cold period. It is at its best at a water temperature close to 15°.

In most countries it is therefore inevitable to use a cooling fan or cooling unit.

For many people, a cooling unit is the best alternative. These keep the temperature consistently cool, even if the owner is not home for a few days. Purchase costs are usually quite high, but the purchase pays for itself in almost every case. If axolotls have to live in countries that get quite hot or even scorching in the summer, this type of cooling is absolutely necessary - anything else would not be appropriate for the animal and another pet might be more suitable.

When the aquarium is first filled with water, bacteria should settle in the water filter and on the bottom. These are important for the metabolic cycle and are not harmful. The "waste" that accumulates - i.e. axolotl droppings and dead plant remains - is first converted to ammonium, ammonia and then to nitrite and nitrate. How long the conversion of nitrite to nitrate takes depends on several factors; for example, how many (real!) plants are in the aquarium. At best, the plants should be robust.

If you live in a region with high-quality tap water, this is perfectly fine as tank water. The quality of tap water varies from country to country - and there are also sometimes big regional differences. If in doubt, the water can first be tested for chlorine, heavy metals and the like. Chlorine is extremely harmful to axolotls and other aquatic life.

Other very important factors are nitrite, nitrate and ammonia. Ammonia or ammonium is formed in the tank water by food residues, dead plant parts *etc.* Then nitrite is formed from this, which in turn forms nitrate. How long the transformation takes often varies and depends on the conditions and the equipment of the tank.

The ammonia level (NH3) should be less than 0.2 mg per litre (*0.2 ppm*).

The nitrate level (NO3) should be a maximum of 25 mg per litre (*25 ppm*). Above a value of 40 mg per litre (*40 ppm*) it becomes toxic!

The nitrite level (NO2) should always be zero. A very low value is OK at times but should never exceed 0.5 mg per litre (*0.5 ppm*) (toxic!). If the value does rise above this, the animals should first be moved into food-safe plastic boxes with cold water until the value has been lowered again.

Some axolotls occasionally try to jump out of the tank. If you have an open tank, the gap between the water surface and the edge of the tank should be at least ten centimetres (*at least four inches*) so that the animals cannot jump out. Otherwise, of course, a cover made of solid wire can help.

Once you have cleaned the tank, washed the substrate and added the tank water, the tank is not yet ready for the axolotl. First of all, there is what is known as a cycling phase.

After about one day, the cold-water plants can be added. After that, however, the values have to settle down before the axolotls can move in. This cycling phase can last up to eight weeks. It always depends on the water values, which should be tested regularly until a healthy and species-appropriate bacterial fauna has been established. When the water values have settled in the range described above, the animals can move into their new home.

During this phase, it may happen that the plants weaken somewhat or even die off partially, as the nutrient balance in the tank is not yet optimal. This is not a problem. If necessary, the plants can be replaced or supplemented after the cycling phase has been completed.

Opinions are also divided on the duration of the cycling phase. Some breeders say four weeks is enough, others recommend at least six to eight weeks. In case of doubt, it is of course better to let the phase run too long than too short, to be sure that the water quality is good enough and the balance has settled down.

When the nitrite peak occurs is difficult to predict and very dependent on the individual conditions in the tank. In most cases, however, the peak occurs between the second and the sixth week of the cycling phase. It usually lasts about a week.

Water hardness should be about 21 °fH to 35 °fH (210 ppm to 350 ppm). It should not fall below 14 °fH (140 ppm).

Carbonate hardness (alkalinity) should be above 8 °fH (90 ppm). It is ideal between 8 °fH and 17 °fH (90 ppm and 180 ppm).

The pH value should be between 7 and 8; a pH value between 6.5 and 6.9 is also fine. In general, most breeders recommend a pH value between 7.0 and 7.5.

Some axolotls occasionally try to jump out of the aquarium. If you have an open aquarium, the space between the water surface and the edge of the aquarium should be at least ten centimeters so that the animals cannot jump out. Otherwise, of course, a lid made of solid wire can help.

The water level should be at least twenty to thirty centimeters (at least eight to twelve inches). It also depends on how big the aquarium is in general. Each axolotl should have at least 60-100 gallons of water available (at least 16-26 gallons per axolotl). The more water there is in the aquarium, the better the biological and bacterial balance. It is therefore better to let in too much water than too little. However, it is advisable-regardless of whether you have a lid or not-to leave an air space of about ten inches, because axolotls like to swim on the surface and put their little heads out of the water.

After cleaning the aquarium, washing the substrate and adding water, the aquarium is not yet ready for axolotls. First, there is what is known as the cycling phase.

After a day or so, you can add the cold water plants. After that, however, the values must stabilize before the axolotls can move in. This cycling phase can last up to eight weeks. It always depends on the water values, which must be checked regularly until a healthy bacterial fauna suitable for the species has been established. When the water values have stabilized in the range described above, the animals can move to their new home.

During this phase, it may happen that the plants weaken a bit or even partially die, because the nutrient balance in the aquarium is not yet optimal. This is not a problem. If necessary, plants can be replaced or supplemented after the cycling phase has been completed.

Opinions are also divided on the length of the cycling phase. Some breeders say four weeks is sufficient, others recommend at least six to eight weeks. When in doubt, it is obviously better to make the phase last too long than too short, to be sure that the water quality is good enough and the balance has stabilized. The water filter should also already be running during this phase. Plants should have already moved into their new home, as they are essential to the water values and balance to be achieved.

It is advisable to check the water values regularly from the second week onwards. The nitrite value will rise sharply and reach a so-called peak. As explained before, the nitrite value should always be around zero. In the cycling phase, however, it can increase abruptly and even reach a value of 1. This is then the peak. When the nitrite value has reached zero again, the axolotls can move to their new home. If you want to accelerate the reduction of the nitrite value, you can add small amounts of the following to the aquarium water.

Aquarium bottom

The aquarium bottom is a very common topic of discussion in the axolotl community. Unfortunately, it often happens that axolotls swallow small or large stones on the bottom because they are "sucking snappers". Whether this is harmful depends on the size and number of objects swallowed. Clogging can occur, sometimes unfortunately fatal.

In Germany, clear pebbles are recommended as substrate. Pebbles should not be artificially colored. Black gravel and/or plastic-covered gravel should be avoided in particular, as it is toxic to axolotls if swallowed and can also poison the water. In addition, many black stones also emit iron. A size of one millimeter to three millimeters is the standard in Germany. The edges should not be sharp but rounded. Larger stones can lead to blockages and often cannot be ejected.

However, in English-speaking countries such as the United States, the use of pebbles is not recommended. It is true that sometimes axolotls will swallow small stones. If they are small enough, axolotls will usually defecate them. However, there is indeed a risk of constipation.

A good alternative is to use sand as a substrate. Ingestion of sand is usually considered harmless because the sand is very small and fine.

There are many axolotl owners who do not use substrate at all, especially in the United States. This can be problematic because the axolotl would have a better grip when walking if there is substrate. Also, a film of bacteria can form on the bare bottom and the stability/natural balance in the aquarium can be compromised.

If you use the substrate, it should be rinsed before use, e.g. in the shower with the help of a sieve. If the substrate has not been cleaned, the aquarium water may become cloudy. When letting the water in, make sure that the substrate is not agitated (too much), but remains nice and even.

Once you have acquired an adequate sized container, you need to set it up and operate it in such a way as to protect its resident(s) from the dangers that threaten them: dirty water, domestic accidents and heat.

Domestic accidents include accidental ingestion of rocks, pieces of wood, and the introduction of toxic products into the aquarium: pesticides, fertilizers, heavy metals.

We will see in what follows that axolotl aquarium keeping, contrary to the race for technology that is practiced in saltwater aquarium keeping or in certain sectors of terrarium keeping, is an economical, simple and low energy consuming practice. This has contributed to the success of this animal in the laboratory.

The axolotl is a completely aquatic animal. Its habitat is an ordinary aquarium. Those who come from the aquarium world are in familiar territory, those who come from the terrarium world have to adapt their experience a bit. What follows is valid for adult or sub-adult animals, beyond about 15 cm, which corresponds to about one year of age. If the living conditions described below can be reproduced outdoors, a seasonal stay in a pond or outdoor tank is possible as long as the water temperature remains between 6° and 20° and as long as the animal is given sufficient food. A temperature lower than 2°C is lethal.

Choice and arrangement of the aquarium

If there is no risk of escape, a normal cover is sufficient. As the axolotl lives mostly on the ground, the surface of its habitat is more important than the volume of water. It is important to keep in mind that they come up to the surface to breathe - access to air must always be possible - and that they like clean and relatively oxygenated water. Therefore, excessive water height is more harmful than useful: in the absence of mixing, the water column tends to "settle" into different layers according to temperature and oxygenation level. Thirty to forty cm of water height is more than enough. A tank that is longer and wider than it is high is the best solution. Indifferent to its fellow creatures, the axolotl can be kept in isolation. It is even a way of controlling and stimulating reproduction to keep the animals separate and only bring them together to lay eggs. This also ensures that each animal receives an adequate food ration. In any case, only animals of the same size should be kept together, and a special aquarium should be set aside for them, with no fish, no amphibians of other species, and no crustaceans except for small freshwater snails for cleaning. Fish are prey, and, above all, they disturb and hurt the axolotls by attacking their gills. For a single animal, provided that regular water changes are made (see below), an aquarium of about 60 cm long and with a capacity of 50 to 60 liters is a minimum. In a 80-

100 liter tank, you can put two, and so on, for each additional 50 liters of axolotl.

If simple rules are followed, the axolotl, when properly housed and treated, is an interesting, amusing and expressive animal, which can live for many years and reach a relatively respectable size of about 30 cm and a weight of more than 300 g. Its longevity is usually 10 to 15 years, and can reach 25 years.

The decor and the floor

It is advisable to avoid putting in the tank objects that the axolotl can swallow in its reflex movement of taking food, a violent and blind sucking effect. This is particularly the case with gravel. Any object of less than 3 cm can be "swallowed" by the animal with possibly fatal consequences. A layer of gravel or pebbles also creates gaps where food will sink, then decompose out of the animal's reach and contaminate the water. Therefore, fine sand, well rinsed, or a bare floor, without substrate, is preferable, by placing the aquarium on a dark colored background. If fine sand is used, a layer of a few mm thick is sufficient. A thicker sandy soil tends to harden or become the site of harmful fermentations. On this bare or sandy soil, we install some isolated decorative elements in the form of large roots (roots known as bog roots used in aquariums, which are soaked and left to soak in clean water beforehand) and large stones without sharp edges which can hurt the axolotl. We should also avoid creating cavities where the animal can get stuck and stacking elements that can collapse spontaneously or under the effect of the axolotl's movements. However, the animal appreciates being able to hide and half pots of flowers made of earth can be given as hiding places, which do not interfere with cleaning operations and are safe.

These decorative elements contribute to the aesthetics of the tank and enrich the environment of the animals, offering them the possibility to break the visual contact between them.

A bare floor also makes it possible to see the waste, excrement etc... that is siphoned off during water changes to clean the tank. In a classical aquarium, once it is balanced, a porous soil shelters an abundant and diversified fauna of organisms, especially bacteria, which participates in an essential way in the natural and spontaneous purification of the tank by decomposing and recycling the waste. This is no longer the case in the absence of a substrate with a bare glass bottom or a thin layer of sand. The introduction of decorative elements provides additional surfaces for the bacterial films to attach to, which compensates to some extent for the loss of the soil as a natural filter.

Lighting

There is however an imperative condition for the success of the plants: they must benefit from sufficient lighting with a light quality as close as possible to the solar spectrum. In practice, this means equipping the axolotl tank with an artificial lighting gallery, if possible without glass or walls between the water and the lighting source (the electrical part of the gallery must be watertight). However, the installation of a lighting system must be combined with another requirement of the axolotl tank, because the lighting can be a source of heat.

Axolotls don't appreciate bright light at all and powerful lamps is able stress them out. Instead, find something that allows you to identify your Axies beyond scaring them into hiding all day.

Incidentally, artificial lighting provides the animals with a necessary day-night cycle and possibly a seasonal cycle that may influence reproduction by varying the lighting duration from 6-8 hours to 10-12 hours depending on the season. Use a timer to turn on automatically according to the desired duration.

Led lights do not give off heat, they have a long life and are the most economical in terms of electricity for a given light output, but Led aquarium galleries are still very expensive to purchase and the effect of ordinary LED light on plants is still controversial.

Metal halide spotlights and HQI halogens, which are often used for reptile terrariums, provide the desired light quality, but they should be avoided at all costs, as they are the most electricity-hungry lamps and above all the ones that give off the most heat.

In short, the best solution seems to us to consist of a classic aquarium lighting tube, a horticultural "neon" coupled with a ballast, in a gallery well insulated from humidity, the least complicated, the least expensive, the equivalent of the old "Grolux" daylight tube of the Sylvania brand. Let's hope that we will still find for a long time these fifty years old materials and the galleries with tight ends which allow to use them in a relatively humid atmosphere! These tubes exist in two diameters, T8 (Ø26 mm) and T5 (Ø16 mm). Their lighting power and power consumption depend on their length. The T5 are known to heat less, they are more powerful for the same length, so the advantage is not decisive when you do not want to intensify the lighting, they consume less and last longer, they are less standard. The T8 have a real efficiency time much higher than that indicated, as long as they do not "snap". These tubes have a power proportional to their length.

T8: 45 cm, 15 Watt - 60 cm, 18 W - 75 cm, 25 W - 90 cm, 30 W etc ...

T5: 43,8 cm, 24 W - 55 cm, 35 W - 59 cm, 39 W - 785 cm, 54 W etc ...

A single tube adapted to the length of the tank (or shorter) provides sufficient light for most ordinary plants, especially for surface plants located 10 or 20 cm below the tube. The heating effect is limited, and can even be appreciated by the animals by creating a slightly warmer zone on the surface that participates in the day-night cycle. Nevertheless, it is important to open the gallery to evacuate the excess heat when the ambient temperature reaches 20°C - especially for small tanks - and to cut off the lighting completely when the ambient temperature rises above that. Above 22-23°, you should try to cool the water by submerging or floating containers or coolers full of ice and stop feeding the animal. As long as the temperature rise is gradual, water at 25° will not immediately kill the axolotl. At these temperatures, the axolotl does not have enough oxygen dissolved in the water and resorts more to air breathing. It starts to suffer from metabolic disorders and becomes very vulnerable to diseases, especially since the bacterial load of the environment increases with temperature.

Chapter 5: How to take care of Axolotl and keep them Healthy

While axolotls are generally strong to slight variances in their condition, they likewise have sensitive, delicate bodies with porous skin. Indeed, the greater part of their body is made of ligament instead of bone. That implies they ought not be dealt with except if completely important. Also, on the off chance that you do need to move them out of their tank, do as such with a fine work net that won't ensnare any of their body parts.

When you have their lodging arrangement right, you by and large just need to put in a couple of hours out of each week on taking care of and cleaning. The rest is essentially appreciating them as a peaceful, oceanic friend. Axolotls will in general be genuinely intense and are entirely substance to move about their tank as they're being viewed by their people. Some will come up to the side of their tank when an individual is there watching them.

Be that as it may, they aren't especially social creatures and don't need any tank sidekicks. They ought not be kept with different species as axolotls would attempt to eat pet fish, and the fish now and again nip at them, also. You even ought to be careful about lodging them with different axolotls. Adolescent axolotls can be primative toward each other, so they are best brought up in isolated nooks. Grown-ups can possibly be housed together, yet at the same time, look out for savage propensities. In the event that a body part gets gnawed off by a tank mate, an axolotl really can recover it after some time. Notwithstanding, it's despite everything best to dodge this circumstance out and out.

The best way to keep your animals free of disease is to prevent it. Most terrarium and aquarium animals, when they are not victims of diseases contracted before their arrival, are victims of the negligence or incompetence of their caretaker who does not provide them with the appropriate living conditions. A suitable environment and careful maintenance are sufficient to prevent most diseases in axolotls. However, once a disease is declared, the prospects are not good, because amphibians react very badly to chemicals.

The diseases associated with these symptoms can have a wide variety of causes and non-specific agents: dietary deficiencies, viruses, fungal infections, bacteria, aquatic parasites (protozoa, nematodes, Trichodina, Aemonas, Saprolegnia). As our axolotls were born in captivity, aquatic parasites are rare. They can hardly come from food or from "crossbreeding" with the natural environment. Opportunistic diseases that occur on wounds are much more common. The "axolotl plague" manifests itself by reddish abscesses followed by fungal attacks. It kills animals rapidly. It is probably a "combined attack" of several agents, fungi and bacteria and requires rapid treatment (salt at low temperature 13-15° if possible).

BD (chytridiomycosis)

Axolotls should be tested for BD (***Batrachochytrium dendrobatidis***) at least once a year. The disease, also called chytridiomycosis, is often undetectable for months, but is very damaging to the axolotl's immune system and makes them more susceptible to further diseases. BD is a fungal disease. The chytridiomycosis fungus originates from Africa and causes an outbreak of chytridiomycosis in the tank. A few decades ago, the fungus found its way to Europe. It is considered the most common and dangerous disease for domesticated amphibians!

This fungus is extremely aggressive and causes mass amphibian mortality all over the world. Therefore, this disease is to be taken very seriously. The fungus is often transmitted via plants and other objects in the tank, especially if they have been taken over second-hand. Therefore, all plants and objects should be disinfected before use. However, BD can also be transmitted by fish, snails and other animals that may be placed in the axolotl's home (not recommended). If the keeping conditions are also not optimal, the chytrid fungus has an even easier game; for this reason, too, adequate water values and sufficient hygiene should always be ensured.

Symptoms of BD are, for example, black discoloured areas on the body of the axolotl - often on the lips or toes, but also in the area of the cloaca, the belly and the tail. One problem, however, is that black spots can also result from reproductive maturity. Therefore, this is somewhat difficult to distinguish - especially for a layperson. The fungus also likes to stay in the mucous membranes of the axolotl. It uses the animal as a host to multiply on.

BD can also be asymptomatic, especially in the beginning, so prevention is important. BD not only weakens the immune system and makes the axolotl more susceptible to further diseases, but in the worst case it can lead to the death of the animal, even if no symptoms are visible.

Another symptom of BD can be slimy gill hairs. A change in the animal's behaviour can also be a sign of BD, for example if the animal does not feel like eating or seems apathetic.

In case of a suspected case, a BD test should be carried out immediately, but even for animals without suspicion, an annual test is recommended to be on the safe side. Visibly ill animals should of course be taken to the vet immediately!

However, the animal does not necessarily have to be taken to the vet for the test. In many countries it is possible to take a swab at home and then take it to the vet or send it to the laboratory.

In case of an infestation or a positive test result, the entire tank and all furnishings must be thoroughly cleaned and disinfected. The pathogens are not visible to the naked eye as they only measure about 5 μm. It is therefore important to disinfect every area very thoroughly, for example with high-percentage alcohol (at least seventy percent).

Such intensive cleaning naturally also has the effect of removing the valuable bacteria cultures from the tank. Unfortunately, this cannot be avoided. Therefore, the bacteria have to re-colonise after the cleaning, which takes some time. For this reason, the water values should be kept well under control.

If a new axolotl is brought from the breeder or taken over from another owner, they should ideally provide an up-to-date BD test.

Fungal infections

Fungal infections can be recognised relatively well by the fact that they cause white spots on the axolotl's body or even white "fungal tufts". These can often be treated relatively well with salt baths.

However, it is important to note that the salt used must not contain iodine.

For treatment, the animal is placed in a separate box filled with salt water. Approximately one teaspoon of salt is used per ten litres of water (*approx. 2.5 gallons*). The animal should spend several hours or at best even a whole day in the box. With this method, the salt content of the water is therefore low and the treatment time relatively long.

Another possibility is to intensify the salt bath. With this method, one teaspoon of salt per 1 litre (*per 0.25 gallons*) is added to the water in the box; however, the treatment time should then only be ten minutes!

Ideally, the axolotl should be kept in quarantine for about a week afterwards, so that it can be observed further, and it can be determined whether the fungal infection disappears completely.

To remove the fungal bacteria in the tank, it is a good idea to use sea almond leaves. Two leaves of the sea/tropical almond tree (*Terminalia catappa*) are added to 100 litres (*approx. 26 gallons*) of tank water. These have an antibacterial effect and also promote skin regeneration. The leaves do not have to be removed, but slowly decompose themselves.

Axolotl pest

Axolotl pest is a serious disease that leads very quickly to a deterioration in health, is quite aggressive and can cause the death of the animal if not treated. Therefore, the disease should be treated as soon as possible (within 24 hours!) by a competent veterinarian. It should not be confused with a simple fungal infection!

Axolotl pest is an infectious disease caused by mycobacteria. It is a mixture of bacteria and fungi. The pathogens are found in the soil as well as in the water and on their hosts, where they feed on dead biomass.

This disease also enjoys poor husbandry conditions such as poor water quality. Most dramatic here is water contamination by chlorine, nitrogen compounds and heavy metals. They occur, for example, when food remains are not removed and these slowly decompose. Inadequate and too infrequent water changes also favour this.

Symptoms of axolotl pest are, for example, changes in the skin, refusal of food up to emaciation, frayed fin areas and general reddening or bleeding on the animal's body. The spread of the disease over the whole body is extremely rapid in most cases and very large wound areas often develop. Home remedies do not help here; the diseases must be fought with suitable medication, which the veterinarian will prescribe. Treatment should not be delayed, as the disease unfortunately spreads very quickly and will most likely lead to the death of the animal. Often a vet will also prescribe healing baths with gentamycin or amphotericin, but this will be carefully investigated and prescribed by the expert vet.

Even with this infection, the entire tank including glass, objects and plants must be thoroughly cleaned and disinfected (ethanol/alcohol 70%). Many keepers even replace the entire equipment to be on the safe side. As with fungal infections, sea almond leaves can be added to the pathogen-free tank as a preventive measure.

(Bite) Injuries

Due to the axolotl's special ability to regenerate, minor injuries are often not a big problem. Many injuries, even slight bite wounds, heal by themselves. However, it is important to examine and observe the injury.

Unfortunately, sometimes an injury becomes infected or a fungal infection develops on the injured area. In such cases, the animal should of course be presented to a competent veterinarian. In the worst case, the vet may have to amputate one of the limbs.

However, in order for the limb to grow back, it is important that the respective area is not sewn up. This is another reason why it is essential that the vet treating the animal is well acquainted with axolotls. After treatment, the animal should first be kept in quarantine until the wound has largely closed.

After an amputation, wound healing first begins, the wound closes. This is followed by blastema formation and then blastema cell proliferation. Once this process is complete, new limb tissue is formed until, in the best case, a regenerated limb has emerged. However, the older the animal, the more difficult regeneration can be. If the animal is already of advanced age, it is also possible that the limb will only regenerate in a mutilated way.

Obesity

Adult axolotls need to be fed less frequently than many other popular pets - therefore it happens that some owners "mean too well with their animals" and overfeed them. Overfeeding is quite common and should be avoided at all costs.

In order to determine the optimal food dose and the optimal intervals, the animals must be well observed. An axolotl should always maintain its normal weight. Of course, it should not lose weight, but weight problems are usually due to the fact that axolotls get too much food instead of too little.

An overweight axolotl is prone to organ fatty degeneration. This primarily affects the liver. Fatty organs and general overweight also provide ideal circumstances for other diseases.

Overweight is indeed a frequent cause of death in domesticated amphibians. Therefore, if weight gain occurs, more fasting days should be taken. If the axolotl still does not lose weight or if the overweight affects only one axolotl in the group, it is likely that the weight gain is due to other diseases. Research into the causes should be carried out by an experienced vet.

It is not only too frequent feeding that can cause overweight, but also too much food and, above all, food that is too rich in fat.

Sometimes other circumstances are mistaken for obesity. This happens, for example, when an axolotl has eaten (many) stones and these accumulate in the abdomen. In the worst case, these stones cannot be excreted and cause - sometimes fatal - blockages. Therefore, it is essential that the substrate consists of very small stones or, at best, fine sand, so that accidentally eaten substrate can be excreted again. Larger stones that fit into the mouth of the axolotl should be strictly avoided.

Abdominal dropsy (ascites) is sometimes mistaken for obesity. Dropsy is quite common in amphibians - and also in fish - and is strictly speaking not a disease in itself, but the symptom or consequence of an organ disease.

If an animal is affected by dropsy, a lot of water sometimes accumulates throughout the body - mainly in the abdominal cavity, of course. There are many reasons for this; for example, a bacterial infection can trigger dropsy. The organs no longer work properly and, in some cases, if the disease is far advanced, have even given up (kidney failure / kidney hypofunction). It is imperative that dropsy is examined and treated by a veterinarian who knows amphibians. Usually antibiotics are necessary, sometimes drainage tablets are also used. Nevertheless, it is essential not only to treat the dropsy itself, but primarily to get to the bottom of the cause.

Axolotls readily accept the food offered and, in most cases, do not regulate their food intake independently in the home tank. It is therefore the owner's responsibility to regulate the food intake and to ensure that the animals do not become too fat. Being overweight can cause fatty degeneration of the liver and other organs. At first it may seem strange that adult axolotls go through such long periods of fasting (more on this in the diet chapter); however, overfeeding can have serious consequences and should therefore be avoided. Liver fatty degeneration can also impair osmosis, for example, and the likelihood of kidney failure is greatly increased.

The older an axolotl is, the slower its metabolism usually becomes. It is therefore a good idea to constantly monitor the animals and to react to impending obesity at an early stage in order to meet the individual needs of the animals.

Axolotl Plague

Axolotl-Pestis is a serious disease that leads very quickly to a deterioration of health, is quite aggressive and can cause the death of the animal if left untreated. Therefore, the disease must be treated as soon as possible (within 24 hours!) by a competent veterinarian. It should not be confused with a simple fungal infection!

This disease is an infectious disease caused by mycobacteria. It is a mixture of bacteria and fungi. The pathogens are found in both soil and water and on their hosts, where they feed on dead biomass.

Most dramatic is water contamination by chlorine, nitrogen compounds and heavy metals. They occur, for example, when food remains are not removed and these slowly decompose. Inadequate and too infrequent water changes also promote this phenomenon.

Symptoms of this disease are, for example, changes in the skin, refusal of food to the point of cachexia, areas of frayed fins, and general redness or bleeding on the animal's body. The spread of the disease throughout the body is extremely rapid in most cases, and very large areas of wounds often develop. Home remedies do not help in this case; disease must be fought with appropriate medications, which your veterinarian will prescribe. Treatment should not be delayed, because the disease unfortunately spreads very quickly and will most likely lead to the death of the animal. Often the veterinarian will also prescribe curative baths with gentamicin or amphotericin, but this will be carefully studied and prescribed by the experienced veterinarian.

Even with this infection, the entire aquarium, including glassware, objects, and plants, must be thoroughly cleaned and disinfected (ethanol/alcohol 70%). Many breeders even replace the entire equipment to be on the safe side. As with fungal infections, sea almond leaves can be added to the pathogen-free aquarium as a preventative measure.

Treatment Options

For opportunistic diseases with cutaneous symptoms, we have disinfectants, which can also be used to clean the tanks after an infectious episode. The affected animal must be isolated in a small separate tank, naked, without decoration, without light, without filter, to administer the product. One can use a 1% copper sulfate solution (2 milliliters per ten liters of water for 24 hours), a general antiseptic such as Ethacridine lactate (marketed under the name Rivanol, 1% solution), or the good old methylene blue (3 milliliters of a 1%

solution per ten liters of water), or even salt (non-iodized salt, without additives, in pharmacies: 100% NaCl sodium chloride): a teaspoon for ten liters of water for a few days, then a spoon for 100 liters for one to two weeks against skin fungi. Among the antibiotics (against bacterial diseases, but not against fungus), gentamycin (used in eye drops) has proved its worth (1 milliliter of gentamycin solution per liter for a ten-minute bath as an attack treatment, then 0.25 milliliters per liter for several hours). A preparation for fish, Furamor, which is both antibacterial and antifungal, can be tried.

Chytridiomycosis A recently appeared disease, chytridiomycosis, strikes a great number of amphibian species, in the natural environment or in captivity. Many extinctions are to be feared. Moreover, some species seem to play a role of healthy carrier, not directly or immediately infected but serving as reservoir to the infectious agent. This is also the case for freshwater crayfish of the genus Procambarus. This disease due to pathogenic fungi (Batrachochytium dendrobatidis and Batrachochytium salamandrivorans) manifests itself initially by skin symptoms that are unfortunately not very specific: small brown spots that get bigger, scarring patches, blackening of the extremities.

Once the disease is declared, the outcome is fatal and the future of the whole collection is compromised. The germ will be transported from one aquarium to another with the material, the plants etc. It is absolutely necessary to avoid spreading it. It is absolutely necessary to avoid spreading it in nature by getting rid of corpses, material, plants or soiled water. The plague is not very mobile and man is probably its best vector!

The disease is not yet generally spread in Europe and it is urgent to try to contain it. It is a danger that will have to be reckoned with more and more. It has already been spotted in the wild in the Netherlands, Spain and France (Aspe Valley) at least. Animals coming from trade, which often live next to other species (Cynops newts, aquatic frogs of the genus Xenopus), or which follow them in the same installations are particularly exposed. It is therefore preferable to obtain axolotls from a healthy breeder or from a specialized breeding facility. It is also advisable to avoid "crossbreeding" between the environment of our aquariums and the natural environment of amphibians. The disease is particularly active in the temperature range suitable for the axolotl.

For all these reasons, it is prudent to put new animals that are to join an existing collection through a two week quarantine.

Treating multiple Axolotls together

Now that we've established that container cohabitants are a no-go in your Axolotl tank, you might be wondering whether it's possible to treat multiple Axolotls together.

The answer here is 'yes', besides unfortunately it's not a straightforward yes. You'll have to treat few factors in mind to successfully combine Axies.

Excessively bit territory is able result in squabbles where limbs are frequently lost and the weaker specimen might not survive. This specifically applies at the period combining youthfuler Axolotls or Axolotls of different sizes, neither of that is something you must try to do.

Consistently be careful, make sure each Axie has at least one hiding area and treat an eye on your liquid condition.

Chapter 6: Mating and Breading Axolotl

Axolotl propagation begins with moving — actually. After a male and female bump and stroke each other's urogenital opening, called the cloaca, the lizards step in a hover in such a three step dance. The male at that point swaggers away while shimmying his tail like a hula artist, tricking the female to follow. As the two move accomplices step together, the male drops a little white case brimming with sperm called a spermatophore. With the female close behind, the male pushes ahead until the female just skirts over the spermatophore and gets it with her cloaca.

Axolotls experience this romance once per year, normally from March to June. With the romance moving behind her, the female axolotl will separately join her 100-300 jam covered eggs on sea-going plants or shakes. Around 10 to 14 days after the fact, the eggs bring forth, and the youthful fight for themselves. It takes about a year for axolo tls to turn out to be explicitly experienced.

The axolotl's natural reproductive season is in spring. Female axolotls usually produce between 80 and 700 eggs, which they lay on aquatic plants. These eggs are not always actually fertilised. If fertilised, axolotls hatch after about 10 to 20 days. Males reach reproductive maturity at about one to two years of age. Females usually become reproductively mature earlier and can reproduce after about one year.

Males and females can be distinguished by the shape of the cloaca, which is more swollen in males during the breeding season. The cloaca becomes a big split excrescence, overflowing symmetrically on both sides of the body. The axolotl is able to reproduce at the age of 18 months to two years, before having reached its maximum size. The females ready to lay eggs are distinguished by their overweight, the males are always thinner. Except in the case of a special breeding program (color selection), unrelated animals are preferred. The genetic diversity of the captive population should be maintained as much as possible.

Spawning

In its natural environment, the axolotl reproduced in spring. Domestication, as often, has more or less freed it from the cycle of the seasons. The laying of eggs can occur at any time, as soon as both partners are in condition. Increasing the food ration in the previous period, putting back in contact animals of both sexes living separately until then, lowering temporarily the temperature to 12-14° for a few days or a few weeks and then letting it come back to its usual level or to a slightly higher level are stimulating factors. The intensification of the red color of the animals' gills and the increased activity of the animals are warning signs. The females take an unusual pause, tail up.

The males follow the females and touch the tail and cloacal area of the females with their snout. This corresponds to an exchange of pheromones, scent particles that inform the axolotls about the reproductive status of their partner. It has often been reported that the claws, normally gray or white, become black.

There is no mating. Breeding occurs mostly at night. The male deposits small gelatinous packets of seeds called spermatophores on the ground. The female collects them with her cloaca and fertilizes. This merry-go-round, interspersed with pauses, can last several hours. The emission of the eggs occurs 12 to 15 hours after the fertilization. The number of eggs varies from one clutch to another and according to the size and condition of the animal. One clutch usually contains between 50 and 150 eggs and clutches may be laid over several days. The eggs are weakly adhesive and deposited on the elements of the decor, or, preferably - it is also the most practical for us - on the strands of floating plant type Naja or Myriophyllum. There are no really constituted cords or clusters. The eggs are generally isolated. They are made up of a gray or white central core, according to whether the animals are pigmented or not, surrounded by a translucent jelly contained in a transparent shell. They swell after their emission, passing from 2 mm to a little less than 1 cm in diameter. The "germ" in the center of the egg is subject to intense cell division. The shape lengthens, the embryo takes the shape of a comma, the head begins to differentiate after 5-6 days, the mouth around the 12th day. The gills become visible.

If the eggs are more or less respected, the larvae will certainly be eaten by the parents after hatching. It should be kept in mind that the breeding of larvae will require a lot of space (to raise 50 larvae to a size of about 10 cm, three or four small tanks and two tanks of about 1 m.) and a lot of live food, and that it is not always easy to place the animals resulting from its reproduction. It is therefore not really advisable to keep hundreds of eggs. On the other hand it is rather rare to manage to raise all the eggs to the end. All the eggs do not hatch. Especially for the forms afflicted with a conflicting genetic heritage (albino, gold, copper). There are losses at each stage of growth, even if it is the pride of the breeder to limit them to the maximum.

At this stage, a few hours after the laying, if you want to raise the young, it is advisable either to transfer the eggs with the plants to which they adhere in separate tanks, or to remove the parents if you have installed the breeders on purpose in a laying tank which will be used at the beginning of the rearing of the young. No lighting on the breeding tank during the incubation of the eggs. It is advantageous to transfer the eggs in small quantities, between 10 and 20 per tank, in several small tanks of 20 to 30 liters. This divides the risk and facilitates further handling. Once the eggs have been isolated, special care should be taken to keep the water clean and aired. Remove moldy or non-developing eggs and make frequent water changes with prepared water at temperature. The use of an air filter is almost mandatory. Some breeders use an antiseptic (Rivanol, in low concentration) as a preventive measure to avoid moldy eggs. The tank can be bare, except for the plants that have been used as egg-laying support. The eggs can be kept in the upper range of temperatures accepted by the axolotl, around 20° or even a little above. However, they can also incubate (albeit more slowly) at lower temperatures, between 15 and 20°, and it is easier to keep the water clean and aerated at this temperature.

Looking After Axolotl Larvae

Axolotl hatchlings are similarly as curious looking as grown-up axolotl. They are about 0.5 inches long when they incubate and won't move for the initial 2 to 3 days. This is on the grounds that they have some egg yolk still in their stomachs that they feed off for the initial 46-72 hours of their brought forth lives. Try not to be frightened by their absence of development, the most exceedingly terrible thing you could do is expect they didn't endure and discard them.

Once the hatchlings begin to wriggle about this is an indication that they are prepared for food. They should be taken care of just live food until they are a lot more established. This is on the grounds that their feeling of smell isn't created and they just won't understand the dead food is really something that they can eat. This can be precarious.

How are you intended to discover live food little enough for the hatchlings to eat?

Moina and recently brought forth saline solution shrimp are the perfect little live foods for the recently incubated hatchlings. Whatever else might be difficult for them to get until they begin to create legs.

On the off chance that you are uncertain if another live food alternative is proper for the hatchlings, check with the pet store before making a buy. Neglecting to give the hatchlings the correct food can bring about them eating one another. Not what we were going for!

The rearing of the larvae

The first few weeks of larval rearing, until the time when the larvae will accept common foods and then inert foods, are the most delicate time for the success of axolotl reproduction. It is necessary to have an abundance of live food. The amateur who passes this point has done his schooling to succeed in other reproductions of newts and salamanders.

Like many very young urodeles larvae (newts and salamanders), axolotl larvae only accept live food of an adapted size and do not hunt. They are content to gobble up whatever comes within reach under their noses. Decreasing the volume of water increases the density of prey. In a volume that is too large, with a water column that is too high, the larvae die of hunger because they cannot find their prey. With such a low water level, the enhancer filters do not work anymore. The breeder has to compensate by changing the water almost daily (with prepared water, before feeding). If possible, the temperature should be kept between 18 and 20°C. Lighting can be reinstalled to help with this.

Feeding the young larvae

The first "preventive" distribution takes place after the water change that precedes the supposed date of the first hatchings. These foods will have been previously grown outdoors in a large container or small garden pond (e.g., 2.00 x 0.5 x 0.4) into which strains of the desired species have been introduced in early spring, and nothing else, except aselles and snails. The large daphnia are not consumed by the axolotl larvae at first, but they can reproduce in the tank and a culture also yields small daphnia. This food is not available in winter. It will be used as a starter and as a supplement during the whole growth of the young larvae. The big advantage of wild plankton is that it stays alive for a long time in the water of the rearing tank, does not soil it and even purifies it (daphnia). However, it is rare to have a sufficient production to do without the live preys of breeding. It is therefore necessary to start the "artificial" production of micro-prey.

Various small preys common in aquaria: nauplii (larvae) of artemia, by far the most widespread and easiest, micro worms, vinegar anguillules, moina daphnia, of a capricious culture. The manuals of aquaristics develop abundantly the subject, the sites of the suppliers of strain also (for example for France: aqualiment). For artemia nauplia, there are culture kits and preparations (salt for the culture solution, eggs (cysts), liquid food) ready-made, common in the aquarium trade. We will focus our discussion on the methods of administration to axolotl larvae.

At the time of the transition from small to large prey, the axolotls are almost out of the woods. It is advantageous to divide them into several tanks, by size, as will be done regularly thereafter, for two reasons. First, it is quite possible that the larger axolotl larvae, as has been proven for other amphibians, emit a substance that inhibits the growth of smaller ones. On the other hand, if the density of animals is high, "accidents" (taking a limb while capturing food) are also more frequent. Reducing the density of animals dilutes this effect and reduces the competition for food, which is also to the detriment of the smaller animals. Larger animals that can eat larger prey grow faster. If the size differences become too great, the larger animals will devour the others. Cannibalism becomes a more noticeable risk around two months of age.

Cannibalism

Larval cannibalism is often considered an inevitability in axolotl breeding. We believe that this is not the case, that it can be reduced to almost zero by not overcrowding the tanks and especially by distributing enough food. The scientific literature mentions a mechanism of "cannibalistic adaptation" in the axolotl, and this is well described in Ambystoma tigrinum and in the Japanese salamander Hynobius retardatus. Some larvae, in certain egg-laying stages, become specialized predators of their conspecifics. They even develop a specialized morphology of the head and jaws for this purpose, and are larger: almost twice as large as the others in H. retardatus. Cannibal and normal larvae are called "dimorphic". The "professional" cannibals are capable to a certain extent of discriminating their prey according to their relationship with themselves, favouring the consumption of genetically distant larvae. They would be selected by environmental conditions, i.e. the cannibal form appears clearly in contexts where food is scarcer. It is not sure that cannibal specialization has a simple genetic basis. The dimorphism could be induced by environmental conditions in a genetically poorly differentiated larval population.

In the weeks following the transition to large foods, and especially around the third month, inert foods in the same size range can be introduced: pellets, frozen foods, small pieces of freshwater fish, etc.

It may be appropriate to mix the two types of food. Known live prey triggers the taking of food, clumsiness in the capture makes the larvae also take the inert foods that are mixed with the others and get used to them. We continue to loosen the larvae regularly and gradually align the maintenance conditions with those of the adults. A 100 x 30 or 80 x 40 tank can house 20-25 larvae of 4-5 cm but only 10-15 larvae of 8-10 cm, about six months old (preferably always with a lower than normal water level and regular water changes, more than for the adults). After a year, the larvae have become semi-adult animals that measure 12-15 cm. This is the age and size when the larvae of other species of salamanders of the genus Ambystoma metamorphose into adults, lose their gills, see their skin change, leave the water etc. The axolotls, on the other hand, have already reached the end of the limited metamorphoses that are theirs. It remains for them to reach sexual maturity, around 18 months and 15-18 cm.

Chapter 7: FAQS

Where Can You Find Axolotls?

Axolotls are also called Mexican Salamanders because they are mainly found in Mexico – in Central Mexico, to be exact.

There was a time when the lakes in Central Mexico were filled with Axolotls. However, Mexico developed a lot of cities and the lakes were destroyed. Now, Axolotls are only found in small canals in the areas surrounding Mexico.

Since Axolotls prefer staying in deep waters that have plenty of marine plants, losing their habitats in lakes has greatly affected their population. That's one of the reasons why Axolotls are now an endangered species.

Axolotls are an endangered species.

How Do Axolotls Behave?

Since Axolotls remain in their larvae form throughout their lives, bodies of water have also become their permanent homes. As previously said, they can be compared to frogs that never develop from their tadpole stage – so as tadpoles, they will remain in the water.

Axolotls have another unusual trait. If their habitat dries up, they will be forced to develop into adult forms. If tadpoles are removed from the water, they will die (since they are not land animals yet). However, in the case of Axolotls, removing them from water will only trigger their transformation into an adult form. That's how amazing this species is!

As nocturnal creatures, Axolotls are more active at night. During daytime, they will simply rest.

Axolotls are more active at night.

What does it do when it's active at night? It mainly looks for food so it can eat. With its slow movement, it actively searches for food in the dark by using its sense of smell. Remember, it's dark, so it really can't see anything, but its sense of smell is really good – so when it smells or senses something (a prey – or a live food) it simply snaps at it and eats it.

Axolotls have tiny teeth in their mouths that they can use to bite into food and tear and chew them into pieces. Their movement when feeding is so fast that they can suck in live animals as if they have a vacuum in their mouths.

What Do Axolotls Eat?

When still very young, Axolotls are herbivorous – which means that they mostly eat plants. During this time, algae and other marine plants serve as their food.

As Axolotls mature, they become carnivorous creatures. Therefore, they no longer eat plants but prefer meat instead. During this time, they eat small insects and small animals and even small types of fish.

How Do Axolotls Breed and Reproduce?

When it's breeding season, a male Axolotl will "dance" to get the attention of the female. It will also make physical contact with the female in the hopes that it will be willing to become its partner.

When a male and a female Axolotl finally partner up, the male will drop its sperms in the water. These will land on the plants and rocks that are scattered on the ocean floor.

The female will then pick up the sperms so that her eggs will become fertilized. The process of fertilization is needed in order for the female to have eggs.

After the fertilization process, it will take about 24 hours (or a day) for the female to lay her eggs. She will lay these in the water and groups of many eggs will fall to the ocean floor.

Although the female Axolotl can lay up to about 400 eggs in a day, the typical number of eggs is only about 200 – which is still a lot. You might think that these will easily hatch into baby Axolotls, that's simply not the case.

It will take about two to three weeks for the eggs to hatch. With the eggs exposed to the many predators underwater, there's really very little chance for all the eggs to survive. In fact, an egg-eating sea animal can easily finish up a whole batch of Axolotl eggs in one go.

Still, having the ability to lay many eggs is good. Even if only half of those eggs survive (or even less than half) that would still mean a lot of baby Axolotls.

If the eggs survive being eaten and are able to hatch, baby Axolotls will have an even greater chance for survival since they can already move (and therefore escape predators).

At 18 to 24 months (about two years), Axolotls are already considered mature. By this time, they have already mastered the ways of living underwater and are also ready for breeding.

What does Science say about Axolotls

Axolotls have a great contribution to science because scientists use them as model organisms. As you know, animals are used for research so that medicines for humans can be developed.

It has been found that Axolotls are easier to breed in captivity than other species of Salamanders – so that's good. If they can be bred, then there will be a lot of animals that can be studied in the laboratory.

Axolotls have the ability to grow new limbs to replace damaged ones.

The Axolotl's healing ability is also useful during research and studies. It has been found that, aside from having the ability to grow new limbs, they can also accept transplants. Transplants are important in the field of science because humans sometimes need transplants, such as when they lose limbs in accidents.

Needless to say, this is one of the favorite species of animals in laboratories because they don't easily die. In fact, there are cases when injured limbs are healed and new limbs are also developed – the animal will then have an extra limb.

What is the Population Status of Axolotls

Axolotls are a critically endangered species. Their numbers are few in the wild – so few in fact, that the chance for recovery is very slim.

Since they are being bred in captivity (in laboratories and other facilities), we can only hope that this species will not totally disappear in the near future. They are cute and useful animals – and they have their own role in keeping the planet's ecosystem in balance. That means that all animals are important because they keep our planet healthy. Axolotls are cute – that's why they are popular as pets.

What are the Threats to Axolotls?

Introducing other types of fish in places where Axolotls live will further endanger their lives. Newly introduced batches of fish can eat Axolotls and that will further contribute to their death.

Being popular pets also works against them. If they are removed from their natural habitat just so they can be put in a small aquarium, they will not be able to breed well. Breeding is one of our remaining hopes in letting this species of animal recover its number.

Axolotls and Humans

Now that you know Axolotls better, be a better caretaker for them if you should decide to keep them as pets.

They actually make good pets as they are easy to take care of and easy to feed (just give them worms and feeder fish and they're be happy).

It is also important to put them in tanks with 61 to 63 degree Fahrenheit temperature. This is really important because not providing them with a proper environment can make them sick.

Remember, if you're going to take care of Axolotls, make sure that they are happy and healthy in their new environment. This way, you will help keep the species alive while also making some new friends.

Chapter 8: Maintaining the Aquarium

Maintaining the balance

Water quality must be maintained throughout the operation of the aquarium. The water must be kept clean and crystal clear. The appearance of cloudiness indicates a degradation of the water and the urgency of a renewal. The presence of a bacterial veil on the surface is not abnormal - within certain limits - when this veil becomes too thick, it is also a sign of a problem and an indication that the gas exchange between water and air is insufficient. The behavior of the animals also gives indications of their well-being: when the air intake at the surface intensifies, it means that the animal is starting to lack oxygen. As the water is charged with oxygen when it comes into contact with the air, the smaller the water column, the larger the surface area of the tank in relation to its height, and the more oxygen the water can take in.

Another form of environmental degradation, which is invisible, is the accumulation of toxic substances (ammonium, nitrites and nitrates) in the water, which are produced by bacteria in the process of decomposition of waste, especially axolotle excrement.

Finally, clean water is water with the lowest possible density of bacterial germs, therefore, as oxygenated as possible, without excess waste and suspended matter. The warmer the water, the more difficult it is to maintain optimal conditions and the more difficult it is for the animal's body to defend itself. Surface plants, as we have seen, play an important role in the elimination of nitrates. They also contribute to the oxygenation of the water, while being likely, at certain times (at night) to decrease the oxygen content. Generally speaking, a well-designed and well-balanced aquarium naturally prevents problems. However, maintaining good conditions necessarily requires maintenance and/or the installation of filtration equipment.

Regular maintenance consists of water changes. With a primed hose, the waste at the bottom of the tank is sucked out and replaced with an equivalent volume of clean water prepared in advance. To have a significant effect, at least one third of the water in the tank must be changed. The more densely populated and the smaller the aquarium, the more frequent the water changes should be. In the minimal configuration of an adult animal in a 50-60 liter tank without filtration, the change should be almost weekly.

Installing a filter reduces the rate of change. A filter is a "reactor" that intensifies the action of the purifying bacteria by passing the water over a bed colonized by them. For this reason, all the elements of a filter should never be cleaned simultaneously, so as not to completely rid them of useful bacteria. The filter also mechanically retains suspended elements that disturb the water and, by stirring the water, it brings the deeper layers into contact with the surface where they are recharged with oxygen. This also has the advantage of limiting and delaying to a certain extent the negative effects of a rise in ambient temperature. Filtration is especially necessary for large aquariums with a large population.

However, the following points should be considered before choosing or not choosing filtration: The axolotl needs oxygenated water, but it does not like eddies or current.

Surface plants also do not like excessive current. However, they are the most efficient purifiers we have.

It is therefore out of the question to use the high-powered filters, with pumps that treat several times the volume of the tank in one hour, that are usually offered on the market for ornamental aquariums

Cleaning the aquarium

Axolotl fishbowl or aquarium maintenance is identical to 'regular' maintenance, so we won't go excessively far into this.

The most essential tasks are substratum vacuuming (after feedings and during liquid renewal), liquid renewal (weekly depending on your liquid test results) and strainer cleaning (bi-weekly). On top of that, you might need to prune grows and do algae scrubbing where necessary.

It is important to note that excessive hygiene can be just as harmful as a lack of hygiene. Bacteria are not bad in themselves - in fact, they are very important to the metabolism and health of the animals. These bacteria are not primarily deposited in the water itself, but rather on the bottom and on/in the filter.

Excess nitrate, which develops through axolotl droppings and dead plant parts, should be removed during cleaning - however, too meticulous cleaning of the bottom and filter should be avoided, as you may run the risk of eliminating all "good" bacteria.

When the filter is cleaned, it is first emptied. Simply squeeze the sponges slightly. The filter housing is cleaned and, if necessary, the substrate is refilled. The hoses should also be cleaned briefly; then the filter can be reassembled and put into operation. The filter should not be out of service for more than an hour - but cleaning usually does not take that long.

It is recommended to do a rough cleaning of the tank about every two weeks. The major cleaning only needs to be done about every four months.

During the rough cleaning, the plants as well as the accessories are removed from the tank. The bottom is vacuumed, for example with a substrate cleaner (hose). The plants are washed under running water. Depending on the size of the respective plant, this can be done under a tap or in the shower. The objects are also washed under running water and ideally wiped down briefly. During the rough cleaning, the axolotls can remain in the tank; they do not necessarily have to be taken out. It is recommended to change about 30 to 40 percent of the water.

However, during the major cleaning every four months, the axolotls must be removed from the tank. They can wait during the cleaning in boxes that have been filled with cold water beforehand. The objects and plants are also removed from the tank. The filter is then switched off and removed.

It is important to note that excessive hygiene can be just as harmful as a lack of hygiene. Bacteria are not bad per se - in fact, they are very important for the metabolism and health of the animals. These bacteria mainly do not settle in the water itself, but rather at the bottom and at/in the filter.

Excess nitrate, which develops through the droppings of the axolotls and through dead plant parts, should be removed during cleaning - however, too meticulous cleaning of the bottom and the filter should be avoided, as one can run the risk of eliminating all "good" bacteria.

When the filter is cleaned, it is first emptied. It is sufficient to lightly squeeze out the sponges. The housing of the filter is cleaned and, if necessary, substrate is refilled. The hoses should also be cleaned briefly; then the filter can be reassembled and put into operation. The filter should not be out of operation for more than an hour - but cleaning usually does not take that long anyway.

Conclusion

Thank you for making it to the end of this book. The axolotl – a types of salamander – is basically jeopardized and local just to Mexico City's Lake Xochimilco. Be that as it may, hostage populaces are flourishing in labs around the globe, as specialists study the axolotl's uncommon capacity to regrow entire appendages, pieces of mind, and portions of spinal line when harmed.

Most axolotls live between ten and twenty years. Occasionally, however, some axolotls have been known to live up to 25 years. Axolotls need fresh, oxygen-rich water. They are not solitary animals and should therefore be kept at least in pairs. Many owners decide to keep three animals. These should be about the same size!

Axolotls have external gills and their lungs are not fully developed. Although they can go from water to land for short periods, they should spend their lives in water because they are not adult salamanders but remain in the larval stage. The colder it gets, the more often axolotls voluntarily go ashore.

Axolotls have their home in Mexico and are not too common in the wild. They live in Lake Chalco, Lake Xochimilco and a few other bodies of water in Mexico. These are mainly standing waters and lakes.

Axolotls are very special animals. Preparing to keep axolotls in a species-appropriate manner requires a lot of time, knowledge, and even some cost. However, once everything is set up and optimized, axolotls can move in and are relatively easy pets to care for.

If domesticated axolotls live in a home aquarium, this is of course different. The rhythm of the feedings is determined by humans and the axolotls are not used to putting much effort into finding food. There are usually fixed feeding intervals and certain measured amounts of food. Nevertheless, axolotls retain their instincts, identify prey and snap at food, quite surprisingly. However, they are not used to life in the wild and know that food is put in front of them with a certain regularity. They therefore eat just about everything that humans offer them and do not regulate their food intake independently. It is therefore the human's responsibility to control the axolotl's food intake, to provide a varied diet and to keep an eye on the weight. Good luck.